# Salvage and Other Poems

A Poetry Chapbook by Jason Mosser

# Copyright

All poems copyright 2018 Jason Mosser
Gypsy Daughter logo copyright 2001 Amy Lynn Hess

Cover Image
CC0 1.0 Universal (CC0 1.0) Public Domain Dedication
*Junk Yard Car*

ISBN-13: 978-0-9718068-7-0
ISBN-10: 0-9718068-7-X

Gypsy Daughter
Tucker, GA
USA

Print edition is 6x9" in Garamond font.

# Acknowledgements

"Driving," *Oconee Magazine* (Madison GA), October, 2005.

"Salvage," *The Mas Tequila Review* (Albuquerque NM), Winter 2014, no. 8.

"Time Beforetime," *The Pea River Journal* (Midland MI), vol. 3, no. 1.

Table of Contents

SALVAGE 1
LIT 2
BLACKOUT 3
CELEBRITIES OF THE DAMNED 4
MONSTER 6
CLAY 7
THE CRIPPLE 8
KALEIDOSCOPE 9
PHOTOGRAPH 10
TIME BEFORETIME 11
GHOST CHILD 12
EXES 14
LOVER'S COMPLAINT 15
ANY NOWHERE YOU ARE 16
NOBODY REMEMBERED HER NAME 17
DRIVING 18
ETIQUETTE 19
YANKEE 20
PILL 21
QUITTING 23
LAND OF THE NING-NINGS 27

# Introduction

Just anywhere you open this book, there's salvage. Things collected—former lovers, leftover cigarettes, a cripple. Things rescued in offbeat ways—scraggly plants, a skinny whore, an old car. Then there's that other kind of salvage, as in *to salvage,* which is what these poems do. They pick and choose what events and people, mainly from the past, to toss into the heap for refurbishment, to be turned this way and that, polished, understood intimately, and presented-like-new. I love stores like that, knick-knacky places, odds and ends shops, and I love books like that too.

The title poem clues us into the collection's whole pitch, which is somehow to save, to save but at the same time, not to expect that anything ever actually will be. In "Salvage," the title poem, the speaker and his brother, at the request of an uncle who is dying of cancer, attempt to restore his old car only to have the vehicle die in the process. The young men laugh, ruefully,

> because nothing in our family ever worked right,
> and everything broke down or fell apart

Exactly. There it is, the perfect condition for scavenging out raw poetic material. Once Mosser pulls this material from the scrap pile of memory, it becomes the means, now newly-fashioned into verse, through which he can indeed salvage something, even if only from the facelessness of time.

Which is not to say that everything in this collection is a reincarnation. Some pieces appear to have had no obvious parent, though, just as those that are born from memory do, these poems similarly seem to want to conduct us through the clutter. The piece entitled "Pill," for example, takes us for a ride on a stream of consciousness roundabout. Here is musing on the very mundane subject of, yes, you guessed it, the nature of pill-dom and its ubiquity in our modern world. Turns out, the subject isn't mundane at all once Mosser starts pointing out its jazziness, or should I say its jaggedness? The best part is how the poem runs the distance from birth control pills to the *one pill makes you smaller* kind of pills to his envisioning the moon as

> one aspirin-sized dot
> of white lunar light

If you can't be made whole by metaphor, and this is a good one, then you should just give up now. You're beyond saving.

Ultimately, these poems seem to want to reclaim something, though this way of going back to the detritus of the self for solid material is also a way of going forward, of course, or at least of going on. The question is, where do you wind up? What does all this salvaging do? Well, it produces this kind of lovely art, for one thing. The poems are like little lifeboats or buoys that keep us above the waterline, as all art does. Though whether the speaker, whom we encounter in the poems, is kept afloat is not clear. As he says in "Any Nowhere You Are"

> sometimes
> where you are
> is a nowhere
>
> so nowhere
> no one knows where

Most poets write to save themselves somehow, in ways large and small. Readers of "Salvage and Other Poems" might find they've experienced deliverance, but a small darkness shadowing these pieces hints that maybe the persona has not.

- Susan Azar Porterfield

# SALVAGE

My brother and I drove downtown
to pick up a car from our uncle Lou,
a rusted and busted red Ford Falcon
Lou wanted my brother to repaint and repair.

Aunt Betty showed us into the living room,
dimly lit by an artificial green Christmas tree,
and our uncle Lou, Navy vet, World War Two,
the brightness of his promise long since darkened by drink,
greeted us in one of Betty's old flannel nightgowns.
He was sick with cancer and he was dying,
and embarrassed and apologetic about his appearance,
but neither Cam nor I pretended to notice,
just left with the keys and our Merry Christmases

I drove the Falcon, my brother behind in the Buick,
and as we crossed the Kanawha River
the Falcon started to sputter and spew smoke.
So, casting rearview glances at my brother,
who was laughing and waving me on shouting Go! Go!
I pumped and prayed and pulled that Falcon into a service station.

And as the mechanic extinguished its smoking carcass,
my brother and I just looked on and marveled
because nothing in our family ever worked right,
and everything broke down or fell apart,
so we laughed the laughter of survivors of disaster,
then we burned it back down that hillybilly highway home.

## LIT

Post-twelve-hour shift,
driving through thunderstorm…
Blue lights in the rear-view….
Sitting on the roadside, cursing,
ticketed seventy-seven
in a sixty-five zone.
Took two shots of bourbon
soon as I got home
Thunder outside rattling,
I started jonesing
for a smoke
knowing
I had no
smokes

Emptying ashtrays,
searching for smokeable butts,
I struck a partial pack
of Lucky Strikes
left by my neighbor
last Saturday night.
I looked to the ceiling,
thanked god for the blessing,
& fired one up.

# BLACKOUT

I can never recall that point
when I pass out on the futon,
then wake to find not one but
two wine bottles gone.

## CELEBRITIES OF THE DAMNED
*For Suzanne*

Baby and I were bored
real late last Saturday night
so Baby said
Let's do something bad
So I said
OK baby
Let's play a little game
It's called Celebrities of the Damned

You take a magazine cover
(I searched through
the enormous pile of magazines
at her parents' house)
like this one
It was a copy of *Time*
with Sarah Palin on the cover
Then I said
You light a smoke
(I lit a smoke)
you tear off the cover
then you burn the eyeballs out with the tip
you hold the cover up to the lampshade
letting the light shine through the eyes
and you get Sarah Palin of the Damned

Baby was amused
so we spent the next half hour
condemning the rich and famous
to everlasting perdition
Donald Trump of the Damned
O.J. Simpson of the Damned
Kim Kardashian of the Damned

So who's next?
Baby said
Your call I said

Who's next to suffer the torments
of eternal damnation?
So she searched through the pile
and searched and searched and searched
and pulled out a copy of *People* magazine
with Jesus on the cover
and said Jesus
of the Damned

I said Oh
I don't know
I don't feel
real good about this

But Baby said
I'll burn him
So she lit a smoke
(even though
she doesn't smoke)
and burned out Jesus' eyes
and held the cover
up to the lamp
letting the light
shine through
then she threw the cover
onto the carpet
and stomped on Jesus' scorched
burned-out eyeholes
and ground them
into the fabric

And I said Baby
You are a bad, bad girl
You are my Girlfriend
Of the Damned

## MONSTER

Was it the look of the loser? The drink and drug abuser?
The gut? The stubble? Do I look like trouble?
A face put out with a poker? A lear like the Joker's?
Was it the weary, wary, angry, scary expression?
Am I a racist? Rapist? Nazi? *Il papparazzi?*
Was it some stench emitted un-sensed by its emitter?
Or was it my hump? My Quasimodo demeanor?
The stiff hair bristling from the lycanthrope earholes?
The bloody stitches in the green, oblong forehead?
The horrible blankness of the blinkless, lobotomized gaze?

Until you are seen; then, I approach,
arms extended, moaning in low tones,
"*Friend,*" like in the movies,
and then I begin to pick the flowers from
your pink and yellow skirt, pawing
and slobbering, "*Friend, Friend…*"
Then peasants with pitchforks and torches descend.

# CLAY

She asked me to sing soft & sweet,
a smoothing song with mellow beat
I can't help it if my feet
stumble & I
stutter when I speak.

*Cara mia*, I can't help it.
My muse dwells with demons
I summon to show their faces.

Should Hephaestus be blamed
because Zeus made him lame?
Like Hephaestus, I swing the heavy hammer
but when I see my Aphrodite, I stammer

for my bride will neither see my face,
nor admire my form, suffer my embrace.
But I am no god, not even a little;
I am made of poorer mettle.

We all come from the same clay;
Say I gather my songs from the shards
of a shattered blue vase.

Our wounds are wound around our fates
& we're born as we're bred
where our spirits raise their heads.

Yet one kiss or caress, *cara mia*,
would soothe the wound
from which lilacs & lilies might bloom.

## THE CRIPPLE

He grapples up the ramp
lurches past display tables
balances between bookcases
hauls his mangled machinery
to the Science Fiction/
Fantasy section

Ovoid visage grey and grizzled
spine crooked like a question mark
he rappels the coffee shop rail
orders an iced something drink
sits sipping it slowly

Pantlegs in puddles around ankles
he hobbles toward periodicals
each step a mechanical miracle
and asks the airy blond salesgirl
in the voice of a fifty-year old child
for the copy of *Cosmo*
with Cindy Crawford
on the cover

## KALEIDOSCOPE

Mark tosses photos
black & whites
on the living room floor:
fragments of someone
with beetle black ring
a curve of cropped hair
eye with upraised brow
and I recognize her
She is my wife

I rearrange her
fragmented features
The spaces between
the pieces of her face
guide my eye around
the shapes inside the squares

Mark scatters more shots I
see her through a fly's eyes
shattered and magnified
half a nose and lips
just a nose
the other half nose and lips
section of cheek shaded
suggesting the slightest smirk

Lips, brows, fingertips
circled by a series of eyes
She looks at me with many eyes

## PHOTOGRAPH
*for Janet*

I said, I want to
photograph you
from every
infinitesimally
possible angle.
She said,
You can't even
photograph me
with my clothes on.

## TIME BEFORETIME

What is the word, or is there one, I wonder,
as my wife rouges her cheeks, sips white wine,
and I mix whiskey and water,
the word for this indeterminate period we spend
getting ready to go out for the evening?
What is this lacuna? This present that,
nothing in itself, exists solely as prologue
to an imminent future?

It's pretentious to say "pre-prandial"
because nobody knows what it means,
which is why nobody uses the phrase,
and shouldn't it be as common as 'cocktails'?
And it's not happy hour: too intimate;
here it's just me & my soul mate.

And it's not quite cocktails either.
Cocktails are drinks at the bar,
in a restaurant, waiting for a table,
or cocktails are what we'll have later
with our friends after dinner.
No one says, "As I told my wife over
cocktails in the bedroom…." Sure,
you can say we're having cocktails,
but it's not about what we're drinking
that I'm thinking, it's about where and when.

It's like before a play, with the actors
putting on make-up and costumes,
preening & psyching themselves.
Then it's curtain call: one final
"How do I look?" "Fabulous, doll."
Then we exit the dressing room
and enter, stage left,
our scene, our city.

# GHOST CHILD

As Janet disappeared into the anti-septic
operational labyrinth.
I walked past doctors,
nurses--all women--
imagined them thinking,
*Impregnator! Inseminator!*
In the waiting room, two solemn, scared
couples and a kid watching television,
a drama about the President being shot
Will there, I wonder, be a bomb scare?
Then Janet reappeared, first attempt
aborted by the sonogram image of a
fetus with its head turned crooked.
Specialists needed to straighten the head
Come back Thursday, she said they said

In traffic, fearing our own heads might explode
from stress of steel stuck on steel for exits and exits,
we burned it back down a rural route
Back home, eyes closed--residual road visions--
I remembered, "its head has to be straightened,"
"its head," an it, a head, *homo embryo*; no longer an amorphous mass
& to think of "it" seemed shameful, offensive then;
and "crooked": my own head,
plucked face first by the surgeon's forceps,
crooking my smile like Bell's Palsey patient,
first act as a human being botched;
but he or she, *fait accompli,* fate decided,
before a single sperm cell swam, egg ovulated,
filed away under *a priori* termination, and forgotten

Tuesday morning, Janet drove up alone,
saw the specialist, OB/GYN, then
called me later complaining of stomach pains
where the specialist stuck sticks to dilate her cervix,
"dilation and evacuation," he called it.

Next day, they anestheticized her,
& the surgeon chatted her up to distract her from
the fetus he surreptitiously hid.
She returned early-afternoon, surprised me at work,
smiling, her body her body again.
Later, she showed me her breasts, hard & rubbery,
like a gymnast's, still swollen from pregnancy.
The surgeon had given her a shot
to stop her involuntarily lactating,
her body providing for the absent guest,
the never-to-arrive, sonogram ghost child

The gangly, green spider plant
brought to us by a friend
from his dank, sunless basement
hangs above the other plants
I picked up from the dreadlocked
Deadhead on Earth Day:
nasturtium, ivy, oleander,
our first houseplants.
We move them from the bedroom window
to the kitchen window
to catch the sun.
And Janet names each
in turn--Lucy, Ennis,
& Julianne.

# EXES

Hanging w/her again,
talking gossip and Armageddon,
and how badly our oddballisms,
our misfitisms afflict us,
and how sadly hilarious
and drinking, smoking, playing word games,
replaying parts, stock comic routines,
and I loved that part of the girl
who loved that part of the guy,
and I still do, even as we try
not to replay out loud
the pain we caused.
We know what bad,
what good parts we had.
Not just the good parts bind us,
but the bad.

## LOVER'S COMPLAINT

Whenever we see each other we drink
We talk and we touch and we look tenderly,
then maybe later I text you, but you don't text me back,
like we never said what we said, we never touched,
we never looked at each other that way
It's true I don't understand why you
don't leave the guy you live with
I only know it's easier for me to say
than it is for you to do, but I still don't know what to do
It's true you never said you wanted me to be with you,
you never asked me to wait for you, but I would,
I have, I do, because I am in love with you,
which is why I try to forget about you,
because I cannot wait for you unless you ask me to,
and yet I do, even though you do not ask me to

## ANY NOWHERE YOU ARE

They say no matter
where you are
there you are

But sometimes
where you are
is a nowhere

so nowhere
no one knows where
who hasn't been there

## NOBODY REMEMBERED HER NAME

Nobody remembered her name.
She left suddenly, like she came.
They announced in the bulletin
that corn-rowed black girl had gone,
who kept to herself in the hall,
worked quietly, invisible.
Nobody remembered her name.
She cleaned our toilets all the same.

# DRIVING

How could I explain myself to this
apologetic clerk at the post office?
How could I explain how much agony
Driving through rush hour is for me?
How explain all the years and miles driving
From here to nowhere to work, then rising
Before dark and driving back in the dark
To and from the nowhere where I work?
The arhythmical motion, the shifts and jerks,
Gravity snags that send balance off balance,
The g-force surge forward, the rude shove back,
The lurching of brakes, the snapping of the neck,
The projectiles shot forward at a sudden stop;
Guilt-pangs of paranoia at seeing a cop;
The suffocation of constricted motion,
The soul-killing angst and frustration:
What does it do to human beings?
Spinning through space in these steel machines?
How tell my defeat and disappointment
When my package arrived but not the content?
The one I fought, frantic, through traffic for;
She said she was sorry, and said it once more.

# ETIQUETTE

Skinny old hooker on Fisher,
top front teeth gone,
gap like an empty garage.
"Need a hand?" she asks,
as I hump down street with groceries.
"That's OK," I say, "I got it."
She says, noticing my shades,
"Everybody need sunglasses,
day like today."
"That's right," I say.
"Need some help?"
"No, I got it."
"Need a date?"
"No," again,
but then,
remembering
my manners,
"No, thank you."

# YANKEE

When many a
true-born
southern son
or dixie daughter
says "Yankee"
they never mean
the Minutemen,
George M. Cohan,
or Joe Dimaggio,
no.

They mean
some carpet-baggin',
funny-talkin',
fancy-schoolin',
union-formin',
delicatessen-eatin',
Wall Street-speculatin',
Negro-lovin' Northerner,
from some grey, windy,
uninhabitable city,
New York, Boston,
D.C., Philly,

teeming with urbanites
of omni-ethnicities,
to whom "Yankee"
is a doodle dandy,
a baseball player,
or a Connecticutian
in King Arthur's court.

# PILL

From the first days of a decade,
when the birth control pill
split the sperm from the egg,
freeing us to copulate condomless,
& in that moment engineered
the evolution of our species,
from the pain-killer,
to the pick-me-upper,
to the tranquilizer;
to the capsule
Owsley concocted,
unlocking the doors
to Psyche's rooms,
her tombs, her catacombs,
as, in fetal form, we curled
up in her warm womb;

to the decade's final days,
that moment space imploded,
when the first *homo sapiens*
hatched from a lunar capsule,
that second we first grokked
a lunar gaze at our globe,
motionless in darkness,
one side nebulous, one unseen;
I watched with my family
on our stereo console tv,
transported to hyper-reality,
inhabiting video images
of astronauts, as if we, too,
felt the solid moon-matter
beneath our slippered feet,
one more punctuated
equilibrium leap,
like the first fish that stepped
from primal slime,
& glommed onto terra firma;

to now,
age of better living
through designer chemicals:
from the attention pill,
to the erection pill,
to the happiness pill,
to the hangover pill;
age of the Octamom,
age of the fertility pill,
chemically inseminating
misfertile housewives
to whom birth control means
abundantly birthing;
age of the abortion pill,
circling the ring
from pre- to post-coital;

now,
when we look at the moon,
we can see it looking back,
we can see ourselves
looking back at it:
one aspirin-sized dot
of white lunar light
illuminating another,
bigger, multicolored one.

Now, the moon is a pill,
the earth is a pill,

birth is a pill,
death is a pill.

Life
is a pill.

# QUITTING

*Smoke smoke smoke that cigarette*
*Puff puff puff it till you smoke yourself to death*
*Tell St. Peter at the Golden Gate*
*That you hate to make him wait*
*But you gotta have just one more cigarette*
                              --Merle Travis and Tex Williams

Because cigarettes are walls,
smokescreens between
where you're going
& where you've been

Because to smoke means not to do
Because smoking is *not-doing*
Because smoking *becomes* doing

Because quitting smoking
means doing things you
didn't do before
because you were smoking

Because smoking regulates doing,
after meals or on the phone,
the delayed gratification,
the tedious repetition
of reaching for pack & striking lighter,
igniting paper & dried tobacco,
sucking smoke & blowing clouds,
sucking it in & blowing it out,
sucking it in & blowing it out--
the systole & diastole
of nicotine junk habit

Because you don't smoke cigarettes
cigarettes smoke you,
smoke your heart & lungs,
your kidneys & tongue--

all soaked in smoke,
all toked & coked & cloaked
in smoke

To smoke or not to smoke,
to smoke or to *be* smoked
Do not send to know for whom
the cigarette smokes
It smokes for thee
It smokes for nicotine junkie

Because of the nausea,
the nicotine dizziness,
because smoking closes valves,
causes heart to flutter,
fibrillate, blacken, and die,
because it blackens the lungs,
constricts
the esophageal sphincter,
& yellows the teeth

Because smoking causes
mouth cancer,
lung cancer,
breast cancer,
bladder cancer,
stomach cancer,
cancer cancer,
cancer cancer

Because smoking is playing
Russian Roulette,
each cigarette a chamber clicking

Click

Click

Because no matter how

James Dean it is,
how rebel,
how Garbo,
how *noir,*
it is,
it is still true
that Bogart died
of lung cancer

Because tobacco death merchants
hooked me, maybe hooked you too
on nicotine junk
Nicotine death squads
hook teens on sickorettes,
hook those nico-teens
on sickotine

Child psychologists
invent cartoon characters
to hook those sicko-teens
Joe Camel pimps sick-o-teen

Because smoking means
selling yourself
into slavery,
into nicotine junk habit,
selling out to corporate execs,
who push the poison,
nicotine poison,
sucking green blood
from the cancerous carcass

Because smoking feeds
on its own junkie sickness,
self-consuming,
like the flame feeding
on what consumes it
to self-extinction

Because of my stepfather,
whose trail of butts and ashes
littered my adolescence,
my stepfather whose heart fluttered,
fibrillated, blackened, and died,
everyday of his *not-doing-because-smoking* life
sucking skinny little death sticks,
sucking death, sucking it in,
dragging death through the door,
dragging it day after year--
his bony emaciated body
like the silly little millimeter longer
cigarette he smoked, smoked, smoked,
till he smoked himself
to death

I see him standing, pleading with St. Pete,
bargaining outside the Golden Gate
He's asking, Do I have to go just yet?
I sure would like just one more cigarette

## LAND OF THE NING-NINGS

I never saw sky
turn so many shades of gray
never felt cold freeze
eyelids open,
turn piss to ice,
never heard people speak
in those tinny staccato
hard-syllabled voices
going ning! ning!
Ningningningningningning!

Alien to my ears
Exiled here,
in Ning-Ning City,
I have observed the Nings,
lumpy doughy people,
lumpy proletariat, doughy bourgeoisie
who pinch their eyes and noses
and pucker their assholes tight
To the Ning-Nings, all Whites,
color blind means keeping Coloreds
south of the mighty Ning,
down in Ningtown

Because the Ning-Nings say,
We deserve what we have
because we have what we deserve.
So ningeth our Lord, Ningy be His Ning,
who ningeth greed is good,
greed is freedom,
and if those non-Nings,
those southside Blacks and Browns,
try to ninger those freedoms
we will say Ning! Nein!
It's a Ning Thing
You wouldn't Ning it

Here in the land
of the Ningy blingy bourgeoisie
there are more malls than trees
more churches
than you can say ning
and when the Ning-Nings elect their leaders
they select from among
long-haired laissez-faire Ningatarians,
smoking ning-ning weed and mongering discontent,
Fourth Reich Institute Architects of the Ningapocalypse,
protecting Ning-Nings' natural, Ning-given Ninginess,
and gun-toting truck-driving survivalist Ningicons,
hoarding WMDs for the Big Ning-Thing Throwdown

So the only question is which Ning
did *you* vote for?
Here, in the frozen concrete land,
of the Ning-Ning people.

About the Publisher

Gypsy Daughter has been publishing print and electronic chapbooks since 2001. Current writers include Robin Wyatt Dunn, Ron Riekki, Julio Peralta-Paulino, Jason Mosser, and Amy Lynn Hess. Editors include Amy Lynn Hess and co-editor Vicki Vanbrocklin. Gypsy Daughter's mission is to publish beautiful poetry chapbooks by poets who adhere to the tenets of contemporary Imagism.

www.ingramcontent.com/pod-product-compliance
Lightning Source LLC
Chambersburg PA
CBHW061347040426
42444CB00011B/3131